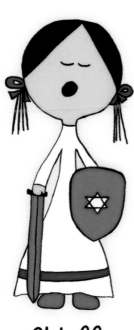

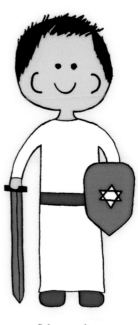

Kvetchy   Shluffy   Noshy

Hanukkah With Noshy Boy and Friends
Copyright © 2013 by Anne-Marie Asner
Printed in the United States of America
All rights reserved
www.matzahballbooks.com
Library of Congress Control Number: 2012945349
ISBN-13: 978-0-9753629-5-2

Hanukkah
with
Noshy Boy
and Friends

by Anne-Marie Baila Asner

MATZAH BALL BOOKS®

Each year at Hanukkah time, Noshy Boy hosts
a party with his grandparents, Bubbe and Zaide.
His family and friends get together to celebrate,
listen to the story of Hanukkah and eat special
Hanukkah treats.

At this year's party, Noshy Boy greeted his guests
at the door. "Hanukkah is the tastiest holiday of the
year — latkes, donuts, chocolate gelt. Come in!"

Shluffy Girl yawned, "Happy Hanukkah, Noshy Boy."
Then she headed straight to the couch for a rest.

Kvetchy Boy sniffed and complained, "Yuck. I don't like Hanukkah. It always smells like oil."

"It's a good thing, too," said Shleppy Boy. "I shlepped this 10-pound bag of potatoes, in case we run out."

"You can never have too many latkes," said Noshy Boy.

Shmutzy Girl walked out of the kitchen, her dress covered with donut jelly.

"Oh, no! The party just started and I'm already shmutzy."

"Don't worry. A little shmutz never hurt anyone," comforted Bubbe, coming to the rescue with a sponge.

Hanukkah book in hand, Zaide took a seat in his armchair. The kids rushed to the living room to hear the story.

On his way, Klutzy Boy tripped over a dreidel and stumbled into place.

Zaide read, "In Jerusalem, over 2,000 years ago, the Greek king Antiochus and his troops took over the Temple and wouldn't let Jews pray."

Kvetchy Boy kvetched, "I don't like King Antiochus. He sounds like a big bully."

"That's what the Maccabees thought, too," said Zaide.

"Judah Maccabee led a small group of Jews to take the Temple back," continued Zaide, turning the page.

"After years of struggle, the Jews finally won," read Zaide.

"I'm exhausted just hearing about it," said Shluffy Girl, yawning.

"Although, they got the Temple back, it was a mess," Zaide continued.

"Sounds like my room sometimes," said Shmutzy Girl. "Maybe they needed to clean it up."

"That's exactly what they did," said Zaide.

"But the Maccabees noticed something was missing," continued Zaide.

"I know!" exclaimed Keppy Girl. "There was barely enough oil to light the menorah for one night."

"Hanukkah would be a pretty silly Festival of Lights without light," joked Kibbitzy Girl.

Zaide read on, "Then a miracle happened. The oil lasted for eight days and nights until new oil could be made."

"And that's why we light candles for the eight nights of Hanukkah," concluded Zaide, closing the book.

Joining them, Bubbe added, "And that's why we eat oily food. Come my brilliant, little Maccabees, the latkes are ready."

The children thanked Zaide for reading the story and went to the festive table to eat.

Shleppy Boy struggled under the weight of an overflowing platter of latkes.

"Please help yourselves to jelly donuts and latkes with apple sauce and sour cream! Yum!" announced Noshy Boy.

Shmutzy Girl said, "I'm going to steer clear of the jelly. One squirt is enough for today."

Klutzy Boy accidently put his elbow in the applesauce. "Oops! Maybe I should have my latkes plain. Still tasty and less to knock over."

After they all ate enough to fill their bellies, they gathered around to light the menorah and sing Hanukkah songs. Even Shluffy Girl woke up for the festivities.

The party neared its end, but not before the kids played dreidel games with chocolate gelt coins as prizes.

When it was Kvetchy Boy's turn, the dreidel landed on gimel and he won all the gelt.

Happy to have won, Kvetchy Boy shared the chocolate with his friends and admitted, "I guess Hanukkah isn't so bad, after all."

"Not bad? Hanukkah is miraculous!" said Keppy Girl.

"It's a miracle the jelly shmutz didn't stain my dress,"
Shmutzy Girl said.

"And it's nothing short of delicious," said Noshy Boy,
licking chocolate from his lips.

Tired and full, the kids left, happy that there were more nights of Hanukkah ahead.

Noshy   Shluffy   Kvetchy

Keppy   Klutzy   Shmutzy

Glossary

A Bissle (little bit) of Yiddish

Bubbe (bŭ-bē) *n.* grandmother

Dreidel (drāy-dŭl) *n.* spinning top with Hebrew letters *nun, gimel, hay* or *shin* on each side

Gelt (gĕlt) *n.* money

Keppy (kĕpp-ē) *n.* head; *adj.* smart, using one's head

Kibbitzy (kĭbbĭtz-ē) *v. kibbitz* to joke around; *adj. kibbitzy*

Klutzy (klŭts-ē) *adj.* clumsy

Kvetchy (k'vĕtch-ē) *adj.* whiny, complaining

Latke (lăt-kĕ) *n.* potato pancake

Noshy (nŏsh-ē) *v. nosh* to snack; *adj. noshy*

Shleppy (shlĕp-ē) *v. shlep* to carry or drag; *adj. shleppy*

Shluffy (shlŭf-ē) *adj.* sleepy, tired

Shmutzy (shmŭtz-ē) *adj.* dirty, messy

Zaide (zā-dē) *n.* grandfather

Candle Blessings

On the first night of Hanukkah, recite all three blessings. After that, just the first two.

בָּרוּךְ אַתָּה יְיָ, אֱלֹהֵינוּ מֶלֶךְ הָעוֹלָם, אֲשֶׁר קִדְּשָׁנוּ
בְּמִצְוֹתָיו, וְצִוָּנוּ לְהַדְלִיק נֵר חֲנֻכָּה.

Ba-ruch A-tah Ado-nai E-lo-he-nu Me-lech ha-olam a-sher ki-de-sha-nu
be-mitz-vo-tav ve-tzi-va-nu le-had-lik ner Cha-nu-kah.

Blessed are You, our G-d, Ruler of the universe, Who sanctified us
with Your commandments and commanded us to kindle the Hanukkah lights.

בָּרוּךְ אַתָּה יְיָ, אֱלֹהֵינוּ מֶלֶךְ הָעוֹלָם, שֶׁעָשָׂה נִסִּים
לַאֲבוֹתֵינוּ, בַּיָּמִים הָהֵם בִּזְמַן הַזֶּה.

Ba-ruch A-tah Ado-nai E-lo-he-nu Me-lech Ha-olam she-a-sa ni-sim
la-avo-te-nu ba-ya-mim ha-hem bi-zman ha-zeh.

Blessed are You, our G-d, Ruler of the universe, Who performed miracles
for our ancestors in those ancient days, at this season.

בָּרוּךְ אַתָּה יְיָ, אֱלֹהֵינוּ מֶלֶךְ הָעוֹלָם, שֶׁהֶחֱיָנוּ וְקִיְּמָנוּ
וְהִגִּיעָנוּ לִזְמַן הַזֶּה:

Ba-ruch A-tah Ado-nai E-lo-he-nu Me-lech Ha-olam she-heche-ya-nu
ve-ki-yi-ma-nu ve-higi-a-nu liz-man ha-zeh.

Blessed are You, our G-d, Ruler of the universe, Who has given us life,
sustained us and enabled us to reach this season.

. . . .

Dreidel Game

Give the dreidel a spin. Either put gelt in the middle or take some out
depending on the Hebrew letter it lands on!

 **Nun** (Nes)
nothing in, nothing out

 Hay (Haya)
take half

 Gimel (Gadol)
win it all

 Shin (Sham)
put one in

Matzah Ball Books®

Products

For more information:

website: matzahballbooks.com

phone: (310) 306-7741

Books

Hanukkah with Noshy Boy and Friends

Shmutzy Girl

Noshy Boy

Shluffy Girl

Kvetchy Boy

Klutzy Boy

Tees

Shmutzy Girl, Noshy Boy, Shluffy Girl, Kvetchy Boy

Toddler sizes 2T & 4T

Youth & Adult sizes S, M, L

Dish Sets

Noshy Boy

Shmutzy Girl